Grant Jones

THE SKOOKUMCHUCK POEMS

Skookumchuck Press

I dream of the dampness of edges receding,
of shoreless shallow and priest-heron,
limitless marsh and altar-bittern;
of an endless mist and parable of petrel,
bent horizon and rain-pale grebe—

    Grant Jones, from *The Source*

In Days Too Long

Once
The boy stood
Among waves feet in sand
Fish around his toes, young flounders
Like pennies and quarters his pockets held from selling
Worms to old men to catch their parents
Down by the crumbling bulkhead
Beyond the point,
Spinning.

He knew only reflected things,
Gathered his senses well
To know each flounder from its eyes,
Each bird before it touched
In that moment when it dived and pierced
The rippling surface of his vision.

In nine years he knew his landscape well,
Sought its breath in the breathing of his walks
Along beaches during days too long
To understand,
Now.

1948 Richmond Beach Tideflats
North Central Sound Sub Region
Central Sound Region
The Salish Sea Estuary
1964

The Skookumchuck Poems

Dedication:

This book is dedicated to ebbtide waders living around the Salish Sea, a salty breed who drop everything when they smell kelp, clam spit and crab shells on the wind and forthwith close their door behind them and hang a note on a nail rusty from years serving that purpose.

Acknowledgements:

I would like to acknowledge many dear souls who walked beside me over the sandbars: Vincent Dobbelaar, Alan Keil, Joe Henke, Ilze Grinbergs Jones, Laurie Olin, Mike Kabush, Rich Haag, Odile Buchanan, Mark Kabush, John Furtado, Ray Belknap, and my tideflat daughter, Kaija Jones. To my wife, Chong-hui Jones, who drove me around the shores of The Salish Sea and shared the helm of our John Alden 1935 Lobster Trawler Cruiser *"High Seas,"* exploring bays and passages and sharing endless nights as we crossed from West Sound to Crane Island in our George Losvar 1938 one-lunger Mukilteo Skiff, *"Krauklis,"* from 2000 to 2007, for these tidewater journeys of discovery, I owe my heart.

ISBN-13: 978-0-9796495-9-2

Copyright © 2017 by Skookumchuck Press and Grant Jones
All rights reserved. No part of this book may be used or reproduced in any manner whatsoever without written permission from the Publisher, except in the case of brief quotations embodied in critical articles and reviews.

Author's Note:
Poems for this limited edition were selected at Coyote Springs Farm in the mouth of the canyon of the Little Mosquito north of Tonasket in Okanogan County. This little book was assembled at the suggestion of a couple inveterate old saltwater beach kids, Jerry and Victoria Jones, farmers now who sequester with their extended family at Indian Springs in the canyon of Aeneas Creek south of Tonasket...many thanks! To my good friend Walter Henze, co-founder with me of Okanogan Land Trust's Poetry Potlucks over the last eight years and co-editor of *Okanogan Poems Volume 3,* I extend profound thanks for his design and management skills to expedite the printing and distribution of this book through the CreateSpace Team at Amazon.

Grant Jones

Skookumchuck Press
Pioneer Square
Jones & Jones, Ltd., 105 S. Main Street, Suite 300, Seattle, WA 98104

Preface

Monster of the Deep

It was early August in 1953 at Richmond Beach. I was rowing out after breakfast on the high tide to drift along the drop off about a half-mile out. I caught a big English Sole fourteen inches long on a strip of frozen herring. As the tide ebbed out and the farthest-out sandbars came into sunlight, I came up with a plan.

I wanted to find out if there were still big Halibut in Puget Sound. In my fishbox I carried a huge halibut hook four inches on the shank. I tied it securely with a bowline knot onto the loose bight of a twelve-inch spool of thick, waxed handline a thousand feet long. I baited it with the whole body of that big sole, working the hook through the back so its white blind side would be exposed to the sunlight filtering into the deep. I then rowed out over a mile beyond the drop off and played out the handline which coursed through my fingers, drug down by a two-pound lead. It took more than a minute, maybe two, for the weight to pull that big flounder all the way down six-hundred feet to the bottom below. The tide had turned and was flooding back toward Seattle. I hauled the line in a few feet and quickly dropped it so I could feel the lead bouncing along the bottom.

Nothing happened for over an hour as I drifted southward from Point Wells toward Duffy's Point bouncing that flounder off the sandy channel, six-hundred feet or sixty stories below. Then, almost imperceptibly, the line, which had been holding almost straight down, slightly aft from the bow, started to slowly pull between my thumb and forefinger and then play out ahead like a walking dog toward the west. Was I just imagining this?

I let out twenty or thirty feet of slack and tied it off around the front seat, to see if it was just a snag and would hold me suspended in one position, fishtailing me slightly back and forth in the current. Instead the line jerked violently and the skiff veered westward at about three knots, faster than you can walk. Oh, crap!

At six o'clock, after being pulled south in zig-zags three miles almost to Jefferson Head, past the Degaussing Station, for two-maybe-three hours, I was getting into the shipping lanes heading for Elliott Bay and would be a threat to navigation. This fish did not act like a halibut, did not want to head for the beach; it was heading for the deep canyon that reaches 800 feet out in the middle of this great estuarine Puget River. If I wanted to get home that night, I'd have to give up my prize. When I touched my fish knife to the thick, trembling hand line, it snapped like a bowstring against my cheek. I noticed that there were two, deep friction grooves in the gunwales of my skiff, one on each side of the bow.

With the severed hand line hanging loose in my hands, fear suddenly pressed tightly around me. I started to tremble and the back of my neck felt like burning ice with electric nettles. Had I been experiencing the whole adventure with a friend, this moment would have brought hoots and hollers, but being alone out there was something else, like an all-engulfing prayer, as I fell to my knees out of the wind and felt the warm and fragrant cedar floorboards under my hands to clear my head, as the wind gently rocked the skiff in the riptide.

It was like time had crashed and some huge power of nature held me in its arms. Some deep-channel monster fish released me, but in the process became my friend and protector.

It took three hours to row back with the outgoing tide. After dragging the skiff up the beach and over the logs and heaving it on top of the car, I drove the old Falcon station wagon two blocks up the hill to the house and rolled into bed at ten o'clock. It was still light and I couldn't fall to sleep until after midnight. It was a quarter moon, and its crescent drew a silver line across the Sound out to where I had met my fifteen-foot Sixgill Cowshark, my own real monster of the deep.

Contents

i
Days Too Long

v
Monster of the Deep

1
Cormorant

2
Memory Number One

3
Ecology of My Heart

4
Misplaced Grebe

5
Fishing with Tson-o-quah

6
The Source

7
Half One Half of Half a Man

8
The Watmough Bight Mollusk

9
Raudas

10
The Starry Flounder

11
Song of the Skeena Prince

12
Kaija

13
Heron in Your Shallows

14
Beach Whispers

15
Skagit Flowers for Sasquatch

16
Love at the Right Time

17
Shadows of Last Night's Stars Sijo

18
Homo Tremuloides

20
Whale Echoes

22
Returning to the Drop Off

24
Kissing Cabezons

25
The Mardrona Circle

26
Creek of Waves

27
Distilleries

28
Welsh Origins

29
Transformations

30
Twenty-Glacier River of the Salish Sea Estuary

35
The Author

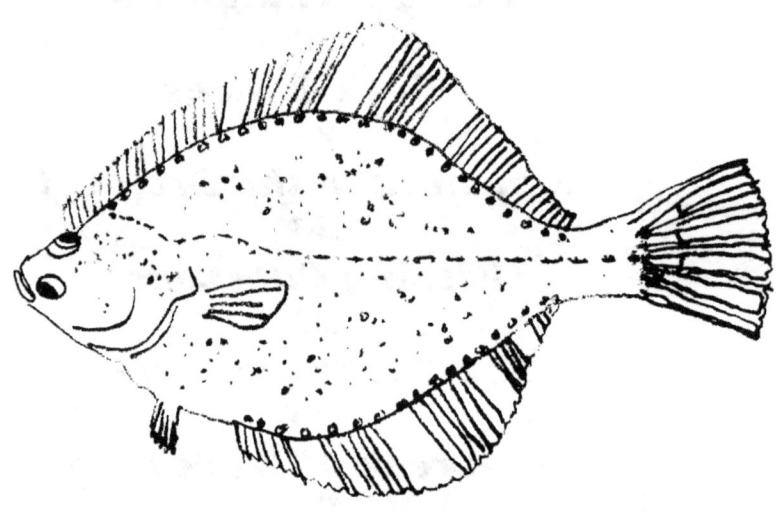

Starry Flounder Platichthys stellatus

Cormorant

On a windy, blowing crest,
Arched and wrinkled brow,
Darkling wing young-feathered moves the air,
Fans slowly, cools deeply:
Cormorant of my diving mind.

Written at Richmond Beach
May 1963

Memory Number One

At three I rolled over my bedrail
And fell into infinity,
Gravity became my friend
And every night for years
I left this world for the sun.

But every morning my long haired Collie
Became my rudder and shadow.
Duke licked back the hair from my eyes,
Pulled on my shirt like a jib
And tacked me through the shoulder-
High grass below the house where
Granddad swung his scythe
In tall breaths from his chest,
To lie down under our ancient Silver Poplar
And look up its trunk five stories
Where thousands of flashing leaves
Roared and soughed and whispered
To a steady, salt wind off the beach
And dream about the clouds that coursed
Duke's orangey-brown eyes as liquid
Messages from the glaciers that hung
From The Brothers Mountain across the Sound.

Written at Coyote Springs Farm
Canyon of the Little Mosquito
Okanogan Sub Watershed
9 August 2014

Ecology of My Heart

When, as an otter
finds its mark
among fine reeds
and weeds of swampish worth,

below a universal brackish surface diving,
you,
in osprey plungings

reached down to prey on me,
to search me out of fish and bittern
dwelling there;

I dived into the mud and sediment
of my decaying past,
found petrified, fossilized,

perfect in all parts:
the shape of my heart.

Written at Richmond Beach, Tideflats
North Central Sound Sub-Region
The Salish Sea Estuary
January 1964
for Theodore Roethke's Advanced Verse Writing Class in Parrington Hall
University of Washington

Misplaced Grebe

Water's flat, composed,
Tarnished ochre-white, fog enclosed--
My refractory vision cone.

Cast over softly wrinkled skin,
Tracing each and only current's scratch
In placid linearity, the birds wait.

While I a misplaced winter's grebe,
Swim out through a coruscating line of fog
Where ochre swells turn rockfish-red
Under this morning's warmth of sunbred air

Bird after bird throws out wings
Lifts each its body trembling,
And flies in a chain through the center
Of the fog's whirly green eye.

Written at Richmond Beach
January 1961

Fishing With Tson-O-Quah
For the Coast Salish *spirit of sea and wind.*

The hull is black the gunnel red
The evening sea sculpin green.
I drift among scrolling kelp
And wake to rest alive.

My handline slacks behind the lead;
Will moonlight prove my choice?
The sea is still in ebbing light;
I wait to see her voice.

The flood tide wind of Tson-o-quah speaks:
Twelve
Foot
Skiff.
My handline glides the gunnel edge
And speaks to me with fish.

Written at Richmond Beach
North Central Sound Sub-Region
The Salish Sea Estuary
July 1966

The Source

I remember cheek-wind hours of peninsular days among waves
on sands at edges whispering with plover
and love in my eye for spindrift, wave lap,
my tracks in the sand with an incoming tide.

I dream of the dampness of edges receding,
of shoreless shallow and priest-heron,
limitless marsh and altar-bittern;
of an endless mist and parable of petrel,
bent horizon and rain-pale grebe—

a collocation of pebble memories
under a curving, white, cloud-hung light
and no horizon to level these senses
or tilt this moment's counterpoise.

I dream of whale-blue navel scars
in bloodless depths of prismed skies;
in mediums of silted time,
to spawn with so much ancient fishlove
to wake without pulse, to listen, to rise,
to dream with gull, wide eyes
At such heights as tears form clouds.

Such nights as these, and mornings—
Pressed against the breath of my beginning—
I wake, suspended
among murmurings of my source.

Written at Point Wells
Richmond Beach Tideflats
North Central Puget Sound Sub-Region
The Salish Sea Estuary
August 1966

Half One Half of Half a Man
For Victor Wellington Jones, 1958-1990

April of 1964, he was five years old, i.e.,
5, of 10, of 20, of 40, a mature man.

Half one-half of half a man,
Sweet small stalk of a someday man,
He, small man, bird child,
Son of a sometime man child,
My child, lovechild,
Loves seashells: that's all I know.

Written at Richmond Beach Tideflats
North Central Puget Sound Sub-Region
The Salish Sea Estuary
Theodore Roethke's Verse Writing Class in Parrington Hall
University of Washington

The Watmough Bight Mollusk

One chilly summer morning in Watmough Bight
I got the quivering milt squeezed right out of me.
An octopus mollusk I hauled up with my anchor
now swirled athwart my Mukilteo skiff,
groped its tentacles across the flywheel,
and choked my Wisconsin one lunger
like an eight handed cowgirl.

Cutting off the tentacle fleeting round that flywheel with my fillet knife,
I tumbled her peering, bulbous body
over the gunnel, back into the bay.

She was stressed a copper-kelp red,
but when water caressed her she flexed like Esther Williams
and sling-shotted toward the drop-off where she'd come from.
I brought her still writhing arm back ashore
and layed it gently on the poker-chip beach.

Immediately it mottled out a speckled, spy gray.
After the muscles lost memory, I sliced it up for sashimi.
I had no octopus ink to soften the rubbery morsels,
so I fried them like cockle necks instead.
I savored this mollusk moment knowing
she'd grow a new, tentacled arm
to hug my anchor next year, returning.

Written at Watmough Bight, south tip of López Island under Chadwick Head
Rosario Strait Sub-Region
The Sand Juan Islands Archipelago Region
The Salish Sea Estuary

Raudas

1

To the barnacled, old dolphin-piles surrounded by cockles
    A heron crossed the Sound from Kingston.
        I miss you.

2

Lost in fog an Arctic Tern skimming waves
    Collided the ferry. Where
        Is your voice?

3

This morning along a riprap wall on a beach with driftwood
    My footprints washed away; alone.
        I'm searching.

4

Some evening's give this forest's windy, cedar chorus
    A doe in the salal, watching me,
        Your eyes.

5

Last night heaved in darkness, my caging ribs compressed the petrel
Of my fear beating in my chest.
        I need you.

6

This evening, the fire dying, I can hear it already on the roof,
    My loneliness dragging its wing.
        I love you.

Six raudas (Latvian runes), tercets, metered 5,3,1
Written at Richmond Beach Farm
North Central Sound Sub-Region
The Salish Sea Estuary
September 1968.

Song of the Starry Flounder

Two arms, out beyond your land,
One fist, thrusts a green band;
Live mass of tide-wrinkled water
Mingles between in plankton laughter.

Four seals ride the swells in;
Three petrels fly by turn spin;
Waves wash in between
Granite cliffs leeward lean.

Six plover dip the wind home;
Five cormorants skip wings trace foam;
Flounder that I am looks on
Through swaying strands of kelp at dawn,
To see refracted cobalt blue,
My upside-down face, prism true.

Written at Watmough Bight, south tip of López Island under Chadwick Head
Rosario Strait Sub-Region
The Sand Juan Islands Archipelago Region
The Salish Sea Estuary
16 October 1962
Theodore Roethke's Advanced Verse Writing Class in Parrington Hall
University of Washington

The poem's architecture is a *trochaic tetrameter with spondaic substitutions at the beginning of the first two stanzas for tension, in the last stanza settling into a regular, relaxed trochaic form.*

Song of the Skeena Prince
Of a shaking, bending, rigid tilting
And a creaking spar-boom swinging,
Huge iron cricket, hind legs swaying
To endless rolls of swollen wind,
Shivering, trembling at the boom tips,
Forestays whining, shrouds hissing,
Commingling in a pulsing, drenched arpeggio—
Rising, falling, mackled sky
Wind and winter moon
Sculpin seas on Hecate Strait,
Mediums of shifting foams,—
Climbing a tall-curling wash, her bow-plates shudder,
Black hull poised before the next pitch,
Moon's pacing, gray whorl,
Evanescent binnacle of the Haida night,
Impaled on crosstrees divining,
And with her spoon stern dripping in a sensual wobble,
Phosphorescence glowing in her well-decks,
The old ship spoke, groaning through her deck vents:
'Skeena Prince,' 'Skeena Prince'
Bound for Port Cleménts;
'Skeena Prince,' 'Skeena Prince'
Bound for Port Cleménts;
Seagirt, lonely, island places,
Bella Coola, Campbell Island,
Jedway, Taena, Moresby Camp,
Village, cannery, cove and mission,
Skídegate, Sandspit, Skídegate Mission,
Queen Charlotte, Mássett, Port Cleménts,—
Brimming host to barnacle and freight clerk
Astral prince of the Canadian night
Bound for the sunken villages of our grandfathers.

Written aboard "MV Skenna Prince," sailing out of Vancouver,
Through South, Central & North Straits of Georgia, across Queen Charlotte
Sound and Hecate Strait to Haida Gwaii
August 1965

Kaija

I heard your cry--
sounds of our breath
rustling of leaves
crumbling shore
our hands in the sand—

Heart
incessant beating
coming
transfiguration of forms
as waves
as birds migrating
seagulls.

You've come
wings
unfolding
closing
the cycle:
Kaija!

Written at Richmond Beach Farm
North Central Sound Sub-Region
The Salish Sea Estuary
March 21, 1971

Heron in Your Shallows

Like resin of the pine becomes radiant stone
From clay you were given you made yourself,
Shaped and laid your own amber shore.
From tall Baltic pines your keel was put down,
But on it you built your own boat, charted
Your own course, found your own voice
In the place you inhabited where rain drips from cedars
On still waters like a code on the beach by the forest
that still mentors you.

In the fullness of autumn
Some flowers just last and last.
I wish I could ebb and flow by the moon
Like the tide, twice daily and twice nightly
To take measure of your beauty.to stand like a heron
In your shallows, craning my neck for a glimpse,
Your gentle figure moving through the tall grass
On the way to the tipi.

Written at Jones Beach on Pole Pass
Crane Island of the Wasp Islands
Central San Juan Sub-Region
The San Juan Archipelago Region
The Salish Sea Estuary
August 1996

Beach Whispers

Wind whispers
          in the pines this morning
                    the way you murmur at first light.

When I walk on the beach
          each cockle shell talks
                    aad reminds me of your smile.

Every time I hear them
          I can't keep from laughing
                    as your voice rehearses in the waves.

Written at Mossy Cliff Cabin
Crane Island of the Wasp Islands
Central San Juan Islands Sub-Region
The San Juan Archipelago Region
The Salish Sea Estuary
July 2003

Skagit Flowers for Sasquatch

Walking straight into the sun
I scrambled across the ancient drift logs,
Some as old as the last Indian
Who knew the Sasquatches who lived
Across the delta on the bluffs above Utsalady,
Walking out into the full embrace
Of this enchanted landscape halfway
Between frogs and flounders and dragonflies
Of the ditches and Caspian terns of the mud bars,
Halfway between this year's cedar logjams from the mountains
And the long banks of driftwood across the shores of Skagit Bay,
And I sat down on a log hummock at the head of a small guzzle
Leading into a salt creek that tracks off into the sunset,
To fill my eyes, now that there are these things
Like rippling sun streaks leaping across the delta,
Like rolling swirls of sandpipers in the tide sets,
Like streaming chains of geese across the bars...
Now that there are these times when birds say your name,
Now that there are these times when the thought of you
Bursts from the swaying grass like a harrier lifting the wind,
Now when words spring from my tongue
Like the flowers you've seeded in my heart.

Written out on the Skagit Bay Flats of Fir Island, which is really the delta of the north and south distributaries of the Skagit River, just north of Utsalady on Camano Island, "Land of the Berries," and home of the Kikiallus Tribe of Coast Salish People, recorded by the Duwamish to be the birthplace of the Sasquatch.

Skagit Bay Sub-Region
The North Sound Region
The Salish Sea Estuary
April 9, 2005.

Love at the Right Time

If I on the beach while I'm sitting,
    lift my foot
    and the footprint holding
    this morning's yellow shade
        harbors a dozen sand fleas
        who hop out into bright rays of the sun
        and attract dragonfly
        whose mate follows
        across shallows along the shore,
        her shadow coursing over the water
        stirring minnows which lure sand dabs
        that great blue heron then spears for breakfast,
and if that footprint contains
    a shell
    which reminds me of the spiral
    curve of your eyelid
        causing me to gulp rasping air
        followed by a long audible sigh
        which wakes song sparrow in the brush at my back
        and makes her careen into the fir overhanging the eelgrass bed
        dislodging a fresh green cone which slowly sinks to the bottom
        attracting rock crab which otter on the bank then dives for,
and if my laughing breath containing all these feelings
    rises to mingle with the summer clouds
    whose billowy bellies you can almost touch,
then I say, what is life
    but love at the right time
        all the way to the spinnakers of the moon.

Written on Crane Island of the Wasp Islands
Central San Juan Islands Sub-Region
The San Juan Archipelago Region
The Salish Sea Estuary

Shadows of Last Night's Stars, a Sijo

This morning six Harbor Seals
Surface below the cliff
Where this cabin rests in the trees.

I stare down at them
Like a captain checking currents.
After they dive, a dozen buffleheads come up.

From Pole Pass
To Deer Harbor
The bay is smooth as glass.

A thousand birds
Are leaving a thousand trails
Across the water
Like rice paper coming alive.

Sky and water
Mirror images
Islands suspended between.

Now, a bald eagle dives, and
They all lift to take flight—
Squadrons and squadrons of cormorants

Skimming across the bay,
Their wakes still trailing
Like long shadows of last night's stars.

Sijo written at Mossycliff Cabin on Crane Island of the Wasp Islands
Central San Juan Islands Subregion
The San Juan Archipelago Region
The Salish Sea Estuary
July 2003

Homo Tremuloides

How far did you blow...was it down from Kodiak...
Before your seed found sweet-water springs
Up the far head of East Sound?
How long had you soughed in the wind
Before feeling the soft scrape of the skinboats in the sand
Beside the sleeping driftlogs from the Hook Yong Jang,
Now River Amur.
How long did you wait on that backdune by the spring
Before our cedar sail fluttered and you fluttered back?...
We flashed our paddles and smelled like cockles that walked.
And for how long had you already unhinged your leaves
Before we saw them blinking and blinked back at you?...
We'd seen so many mirages on the ice.
You made yourself delicious to other animal partners
From ocean to mountain and prairie to muskeg.
But you needed a manager attracted to your beauty.
We began leaving kisses to our women on your bark.
So for how long did you wait, for the steward you made of us?
Your sensorous bark would die by fire, but your roots could take it.
Later our small fires were loving, not all that hot.
After that came your advanced quaking, just for us,
Flashing five miles out, with whispering and trembling up close.
You were perfect for us and we wanted you to have everything.
But the newcomers arrived so distracted they dropped the ball.

Coyote Springs Farm
Little Mosquito Canyon of the Aspens
Mosquito Creek-Okanogan Sub-Watershed
Okanogan River Sub-Basin

Read the notes on the following page!

Life History of the Quaking Aspen in the Americas

At the back of Swift Bay, in the San Juan Islands Archipelago, a long way up Orcas Island's East Sound, an ancient band of Quaking Aspen (Populus tremuloides) grows on the slightly elevated ridge of a sandy backdune, separating the driftwood shore of the bay from a freshwater swamp fed by a distributary of the creek delta behind. How these aspens pioneered this rare grove is a mystery. The road to Mt. Constitution now cuts off the beach-to-dune continuum, but quite likely there are middens still scattered along this aspen-strewn reach of the bay, relicts from a long-standing Indian village. However without the loving fires of the human stewards along the beach, the aspen are being engulfed by firs and may die out in this generation.

The Quaking Aspen came with the glaciers, fifteen to twenty-thousand years ago, spreading by partnership with our human species (we managed fire regeneration of roots whereas seeding is wind-borne). We may have assisted their spread throughout the Americas beyond the Sierra Nevada as far as the Sierras of Baja California and the Sierra Oriental of Central Mexico. Tree groves are dioecious, single-sexed, with males found generally at higher elevations and females in lower elevations and of course they are clonal, that is, each grove is a single individual whose spreading ramets sprout from the underground roots of a single organism. Their bark is vegetative and photosynthesizes like leaves do, making the bark non-resistant to fire, but thus dependent on human-set, small, (non-fatal) fires. Alternatively, after current-day, devastating human-suppressed fires, only wind-blown seeds from an adjacent unburned grove can establish a new grove in a burned-out zone.

Sources: Hutch Brown, "Wildland Burning by American Indians in Virginia," *Fire Management Today*, Volume 60 No. 3, Summer 2000, pp 29-37.

Whale Echoes
Memories for my daughter Kaija on her Birthday
March 21, 2012

Crusader slips her Sitka berth and arcs north.
It's my helm tonight through Neva Straight,
I'm building up grace for the Chatham Straits.

    Ka chunk, ka chunk, ka chunk
      Timeless piston drum.
        "There she blows!"...a Humpback's trace.

Evening falls in Whitestone Bay.
At four A.M. we clear Sergius Narrows,
Then head up Peril Strait's torn clear-cut face.

    Ka chunk, ka chunk, ka chunk
      Sleepless piston drum.
        "They blow"...whale's grace, a dozen.

Crusader shakes her wave-pounded bow.
Green surf unwinds on Red Bluff's face.
Hold her full ahead to slip through a crack,
Then glide, up Gut Bay, to sleep under the waterfall,

    Ka chunk, ka chunk, ka chunk
    Endless piston drum:
      A lone-wolf Blue follows us in to sleep for the night.

Next morning, we're down Baranof, for a dead Orca girl.
Her head stove-in by a cruise ship bow,
Beached now, in the wettest spot of Alaska,

    Ka chunk, ka chunk, ka chunk
     Homeless, piston drum:
      Little Port Arthur, but we call it "Whale Grave Bay."

Crusader climbs green swells of Chatham Straits.
Steer a helm that veers like a smile for Bay of Pillars,
Leave tears in the tide races of Washington Bay
Our sad faces wiped by Earth's pulling graces,

> *Ka chunk, ka chunk, ka chunk*
> *Happy piston drum:*
>   *Whale echoes bounce the moonlight down Frederick Sound.*
>   *It's Petersburg at sunrise for breakfast.*

Written aboard Jonathan White's 75' Halibut Schooner "*Crusader*" of the Resource Institute, and under the command of xxx, throughout the Alexander Archipelago, navigating Chichagof, Baranof, Kuiu and Kupreanof Islands with daughter, Kaija Jones, and marine biologist, Jan Straley, August 7-13, 1991.

Historical Note: In the spring of 1919, my father, Victor Noble Jarrott Jones, after graduating from Ballard High School, came up from Seattle on the "*MV Santa Clara*" of the Alaska Steamship Line, and spent the long rainy summer working the fish cannery in Washington Bay.

Returning to the Drop Off

Alone I went out early,
before first bird cry,
before gulls and fishcrows
began plundering and waded
to the outermost bar
good half mile offshore.

The bar'd been drying before sun break.
I could see that the sand crystals had split open
like tiny mouths above each clam shell.

Each of these refts marks a cockle
with a telltale crack to practiced eyes,
can even etch a string of cockles,
a whole reave of morsels in the ridge of a sandbar.

Glaucous-winged gulls learn to see
these secret messages in the sand
over a lifetime predatoring.
They cock their heads back trying
to hear the whispers from the cockles
as they open their shells a tiny crack at a time.

At only a half inch below the surface,
a cockle will become clearly visible.
Deeper, only a faint double crack
like a pair of eyes will appear.
The young gulls hadn't noticed yet,
but I could see them now plain,
everywhere.

I scuffled across the tiny reaves
with my boot, so any wise old gulls
would have to look for breakfast farther up the beach.

The outermost bar was really
two bars with a lagoon
in between leading to blue water.

There, in the glistening shallows,
fluid in the currents ebbing out <u>through</u>
these two pristine fingers,
there in the dark green eelgrass
that swirls tangled with eel blennies
who tickled my calves as I waded my own path,
as seaperch darted <u>through</u> the kelp strands
startling sanddabs who exploded right <u>over</u> my toes,
the water was colder and the bottom creeped.

Wading deeper, water licking up my ribs,
I begin to hear my young boy spirit
breathing deeply, as I went suspended, bouncing
on the calving edge of the drop off.

But wait, turn around. I was too old for this
and my spirit needed its home,
right here in my chest.

Richmond Beach Tideflats at Point Wells, two miles north of Boeing Creek
Central Puget Sound Sub-Region
The Central Puget Sound Region
The Salish Sea
January 26, 2016

Kissing Cabezons
For Joseph E. Henke

Bull

kelp

swirls down deep

its cadmium ribbons pumping the sun

where greenlings dart

like eels.

Just over the curving

mouth of the drop off

there's a cabezon with cobalt-blue lips

sleeping like a cat.

I knew you'd grow up this serene.

Written on the Richmond Beach Tideflats, in memory of the summer of 1953
North Central Sound Sub-Region
The Salish Sea Estuary
August 20, 2011

The Madrona Circle
For Mike Robinson

We need a "transformer" to save us
now we've wrecked the kitchen,
and our salmonberries have no salmon,
now we've buried the gathering places,
though you can still hear drums
at the creek mouths,
now we've scattered the sleeping places of the elders,
but the west slopes have ledges
where you still feel
their sun on your forehead,
their whispers by the corners
of your mouth, as cool breaths
wreath down your neck.

Sit down, kiss your fingers,
then clasp your hands,
and rest to breathe your dreams unravelling.
K'wati waits with Duckwibal and Musp
and with Sinkalip around the fire circle.
They nod for you to join them,
over there between the Madronas.

So go.

Lincoln Park
Fauntleroy Creek Watershed
South Central Puget Sound Sub-Region
Central Sound Region
The Salish Sea Estuary
February 22, 2015

Creek Of Waves

There's a northwind blowing;
Strings of fishcrows stretch like beads
Across the fingers of the delta.
They strut and poke, flipping rocks, crab cruising,
Squawking at the waves--
Staring down the wind every time it gusts.

Mouth of Shingle Mill Creek
Fern Cove on North Vashon Island
Colvos Passage
Central Sound Sub-Region
The Salish Sea Estuary
April 10, 2010, hiking with Joe Henke

Distilleries

Your firs* take the lead,
their folded-needle flumes
sending billions of cloudwater
molecules down their boles
into the spongey tongues
of moss, french-kissing the creeks
with pure water. Each tree
a distillery of hope to your oysters.

Just passing now
the Bigleaf Maple gallery forests
and swamp forests of the South Fork
of the Snoqualmie River
east of North Bend, heading
for the farm. Sorry we had
no time to chat over a coffee
but next time.

Written after leaving Joe's Creek
Caledonia Beach
South Central Sound Sub-Region
The Salish Sea Estuary

*Douglas Fir: Pseudotsuga menzesii

Welsh Origins

Our souls seem to settle in mountains;
Though our spirits continue
To flow in rivers and rest along their shores.
Since, like the rivers, we are uncontained
And spill our banks like winds
In canyons ebb and flow.

Our minds and hearts come from our brother
Animals: The fish, the birds, the insects
The worms, the snakes, the frogs
The slugs, and all the mammals
From the marmots to the mountain lions.
Trees are guardians,
Animals, our eyes and ears.

Written at Dye's Canyon
South Fork of the Nooksack River
Bellingham Bay/Padilla Bay Sub-Region
The San Juan Islands Archipelago Region
The Salish Sea Estuary

July 1972

Transformations

The eagle in the tall broken fir on the island
Has been motionless except for his rotating head.
Earlier this morning he sailed in with the sun
On an updraft that lifted him over the cumulus pass
High above the mainland. It had never been felt
  in these parts before.

I felt like an island when you walked my shores
Climbed my cliffs, and wandered my meadows
Leaving marks in the grass, each place where you lay
In sun behind mossy hummocks, sheltered from wind;
Everywhere you touched my skin, my island
   wears your imprint.

There are rivers that flow from the same mountain,
That have never seen each other, but then suddenly join,
Doubling themselves and filling up each other,
To commingle as if they knew, have known each other
   for a thousand years...

Crane Island
The Wasp Islands
San Juan Islands Archipelago Region
The Salish Sea Estuary
August 29, 1999

The Twenty-Glacier River
Of The Salish Sea Estuary

10 Regions
40 Sub-Regions
100+ Tributary Rivers

Regions are numbered in caps.
Sub-Regions are in bold title face.
Tributary Parent Rivers in the Sub-Regions appear beneath in upper case.
Those fed by glaciers are in bold upper face.

1. WEST STRAIT OF JUAN DE FUCA REGION

Neah Bay Sub Region
SEKIU

Port San Juan Sub Region
SAN JUAN

Clallam Bay Sub Region
PYSHT

West Coast Sub Region
JORDAN

Crescent Bay Sub Region
LYRE

Sooke Harbor Sub Region
SOOKE

Port Angeles Harbor Sub Region
ELHWA

Victoria Harbor Sub Region
ESQUIMALT

2. EAST STRAIT OF JUAN DE FUCA REGION

Cordova Channel/Saanich Inlet Sub Region
COWICHAN

Smith Island Sub Region
CLOVER

Dungeness-Sequim-Discovery Bays Sub Region
DUNGENESS, JOHNSON & SALMON

3. HOOD CANAL REGION

Lower Hood Canal Sub Region
THORNDYKE

Dabob Bay Sub Region
BIG QUILCENE & TARBOO

North Central Hood Canal Sub Region
DOSEWALLIPS, DUCKABUSH
HAMMA HAMMA & SEABECK

South Central Hood Canal Sub Region
JORSTAD, LILLIWAUP & DEWATO

Great Bend Sub Region
SKOKOMISH, TAHUYA & UNION

4. SAN JUAN ARCHIPELAGO REGION

Bellingham Bay/Padilla Bay Sub Region
NOOKSACK & SAMISH

Boundary Pass Sub Region
COWLITZ

Central San Juan Sub Region
MASSACRE, SWIFT & DOE

Rosario Strait Sub Region
BURROWS, HORSESHOE & STRAWBERRY

Haro Strait Sub Region
SAN JUAN

5. SOUTH STRAIT OF GEORGIA REGION

Alden Bank Sub Region
DAKOTA

Point Roberts Sub Region
SERPENTINE

Gulf Islands Sub Region
FORD

Nanaimo Bay/Fraser Delta Sub Region
SQUAMISH and FRASER

6. CENTRAL STRAIT OF GEORGIA

Courtney Harbor/Jervis Inlet/Princes Louisa Sub Region
SKAWKA & DESERTEDS

7. NORTH STRAIT OF GEORGIA

Desolation Sound/Bute Inlet Sub Region
HOMATHKO & **BISHOP**

8. NORTH SOUND REGION

Admiralty Inlet Sub Region
CHIMAKUM

Possession Sound Sub Region
QUILCEDA, SNOHOMISH,
SKYKOMISH & **SNOQUALMIE**

Port Susan Sub Region
STILLAQUAMISH & **WHITEHORSE**

Sarasota Passage Sub Region
ELGER, RACE & CRESCENT

Skagit Bay Sub Region
SKAGIT, SAUK & **SUIATTLE**

9. CENTRAL SOUND REGION

North Central Sound Sub Region
DEER

Mid Central Sound Sub Region
BOEING, PIPER, SAMMAMISH,
LONGFELLOW, GREEN & FAUNTLEROY

Port Orchard/Dyes Inlet Sub Region
BARKER, CLEAR, CHICO,
GORST & BLACKJACK

South Central Sound Sub Region
SALMON, DES MOINES, LAKOTA,
JOE'S, CALEDONIA, HYLEBOS,
PUYALLUP, **WHITE** & **CARBON**

10. SOUTH SOUND REGION

Nisqually Reach Sub Region
CHAMBERS, **NISQUALLY**, MASHEL, MUD, HUGE, BURLEY & ARTONDALE

Case/Henderson Sub Region
COULTER, ROCKY, SHERWOOD,
SHUMACHER & WOODLAND

Pickering/Squaxin/Budd/Eld Sub Region
DESCHUTES & PERRY

Hammersley/Little Skookum/Totten Sub Region
SKOOKUM, KENNEDY, SNODGRASS,
GOSNELL, MILL, DEER,
JOHNS & CRANBERRY

The Author

Grant Jones was born August 29th 1938. He grew up on a small farm at Richmond Beach in the northern reaches of the Central Puget Sound Region of the Salish Sea Estuary to a Welsh-Irish Canadian father and a Quaker English/Irish-American mother. He began writing poetry at the age of eleven, but found his unique voice as one of Theodore Roethke's poets in the fabled Advanced Verse writing class that Roethke conducted from 1961 to 1964 when he was Poet in Residence at the University of Washington. Jones is Founding Principal of Jones & Jones Architects, Landscape Architects and Planners, Ltd., with Ilze Jones in 1969 and Johnpaul Jones in 1972, maintaining an international design practice in the historic Globe Building in Pioneer Square over the last forty-five years. Since 2006 he has made his home in the North Okanogan Valley in North Central Washington, where he and his wife Chong-hui have created the Jones Gardens at Coyote Springs Farm at the mouth of the canyon of the Little Mosquito between Tonasket and Oroville.

His landscape poetry is recognized as a fundamental part of his intrinsic design approach and integral to his research and scholarship in landscape architecture, ecological design and landscape conservation planning. He is an Affiliate Professor in the Department of Landscape Architecture at the College of Built Environment of the University of Washington in Seattle, and has held teaching positions at Harvard, the University of Oregon, UC Berkeley, University of Virginia and Texas A&M, and has lectured at over thirty-five universities on ecological design, landscape planning and poetry. He is the recipient of over thirty design awards including the Richard Neutra Medal, the President's Award for Excellence and the first Firm of the Year Award bestowed by the ASLA. He is a Frederick Sheldon Fellow of Harvard University and a Glimcher Fellow of the Knowland School of Architecture at The Ohio State University. He was inducted to the Roll of Honor at the College of Built Environments at the University of Washington in April of 2015. He was the recipient of the first LAF Medal at the Landscape Architecture Foundation's 50th Anniversary in June of 2016 in recognition of his vision and leadership as Director of Education and for launching the Olmsted Scholarships.

Several poems in this collection have been published in: *What Rocks Know selected poems of Grant Jones; Okanogan Poems Volume 1, Okanogan Poems Volume 2, and Okanogan Poems Volume 3,* Skookumchuck Press*; The Fullness,* Landscape Journal*; Seeing, Where Logic and Feelings Meet,* Landscape Architecture Magazine*; Grant Jones: A Plan for Puget Sound,* Princeton Architectural Press Sourcebook 4 by Jane Amidon; *The Methow Naturalist.*; and *Naming Water 48 Poems by Grant Jones and Mike Robinson, Skookumchuck Press. Listening to the Voice of the Earth,* a sequential journal of stories, sketches and poems presenting design guidelines and strategies for stewardship and community action will be published in 2018 by George F. Thompson publishing.

36

www.ingramcontent.com/pod-product-compliance
Lightning Source LLC
Chambersburg PA
CBHW060427200426
43193CB00056BA/2907